Alice

Jane Weir

Templar Poetry

First Published 2006 by Templar Poetry

Fenelon House,
Kingsbridge Terrace
Dale Road, Matlock, Derbyshire
DE4 3NB

www.templarpoetry.co.uk

ISBN 0-9550023-3-8

Typeset by Pliny
Graphics by Palloma Violet
Printed and bound in India

For Jonathan and James

ACKNOWLEDGEMENTS

Acknowledgments are due to the editors of the following publications in which some of these poems first appeared: Frogmore Papers Anthology: 2005 (*Curio*), The Way I Dressed During The Revolution, Templar Poetry: 2005 *(Mothering)*
Thanks to Séan for the loan of his overcoat.

CONTENTS

AT BENNETT'S

I place this book
as if it were a stake
on a roulette table.
We could be in the Leubronn,
instead of a crowded
coffee shop in Derby.
I say, I want to live
like this - at this pitch,
and I fumble with these pages,
sinking my fingers
into the layers of their lives.
You hold my gaze
like a handful of Napoleons,
smile knowingly,
before clapping your hands,
sweeping your arms through
tingles of air like a concierge.

ALICE

We traipse along the sluggish Derwent,
lug our bags, hessian flour sacks
stashed with second hand clothes.
It's been a long day on the market
with only half the stock sold.
Ahead, three or four gulls, black backed,
snip at the swollen lips of the river.
Not quite a colony, they've turned
themselves in to the land,
to ride out rough weather.
These days we all flaunt
the protocol of the river bank.
It's rhythms launder, can never erase,
relieve this century of its stains.
Banners of cormorants declare themselves.
We are careful to acknowledge them.

BURNING RAGS ON PEAR STREET

My time, the others have gone to ground,
donned their hats, turned up their collars,
stashed documents into the linings
of their overcoats, sunk like a U-boat
into the grey swell.
Time to join my house, sit-in on the street.
Squatting over the grate, I stoke the coals,
sink down into a nursing chair,
listen to the nagging tick of the clock
and nit pick as to who I did or did not do right by.
I spy mice, burnt almonds they scuttle
from behind the split in the skirting.
It chills me, watching them swill their whiskers
in front of the fire, inches from the trap.
They scatter like iron filings when I shift
my feet, reach, search for the dolly bag.
I take out a wad of sodden bandages,
slow burn a weeks worth of jam rags,
slake the damp mouldering with slack,
and think of nothing.

MOTHERING

When I've set up shop and I'm stood behind the counter
they come, the absolutist pacifists, socialist, suffragettes,
the obviously unfit, their faces pinched and frozen,
caught up in an avalanche, an impasse of white feathers.

Out of the Derby gloom their expressions loom.
I wait on their words, their hand and facial gestures.
I recognise these lot all added up are the total sum of mine.
Usually, they ask me the basics, whereabouts

of my terraced house, the chances of a set
of lice free clothes, bed for the night, a scalding cup
of tea. Later when the shops shut up, doors bolted,
they huddle, hushed voices around the table,

discuss which passage they're on, the risks involved
in obtaining a set of false documents.
Later when all is silent I think of them
long gone. A husk of hares, sabreing across
wounds of fields, hoards of contacts
racing through their blood like viruses.

CHANCE MEETING

Everything's the same.
Impoverished light
spreads itself thinly down the passage.
I am certain, unmoveable,
despite everything...
An Irish voice descends,
softly mizzles over me.
Only the boot
persuades me to raise my head.
She claims to know me.
I put her right.
though she tries to tamper
with my words like evidence.
Her equine eyes blacken,
smoulder like thatch.
A screw stands between us.

A PAN OF POTATO HASH

I remember the pan
cheap and pitted
with an age of stirring.
I can see her hands,
licked with damson burns
healing, as she carried
it two handed because
of its dense weight.

And from the tipped lid,
steam escaping,
a yard dog whimpering
by a stunted bush.
Then the sound
of her calling a battered
name from over
a brick partition,
the stiff lifting of a latch.

I see clear, a face,
that I won't describe.
Though something
nourishing, passed
steady between them.

SCARF 1908

We took it to the wall,
milked it relentlessly,
that colour scheme, those stripes.
With open arms, we welcomed
retailers, entrepreneurs,
watched them swarm
like Hamelin rats
around the bandwagon.
We didn't miss a trick
and ate our bread
from off the spin-offs,
warmed our toes
on the gimmicks
of donated hearth coals.

We never stopped,
all the while negotiating
from the upper floors,
as the glitz fell into the food hall
spangling our hair, dusting
the slopes of our shoulders.
Still we didn't start a fistfight,
instead we offered them cake,
a slice of it mind, not a whole,

with a few licks of icing;
just enough to give a taster.

And it was funny
because what we thought
was a fluke turned out
to be the star surprise,
an early device we'd dreamt up
of purple, green and white,
that proved like a triple-decker,
to be our best seller, smashing
all records for utility silk.

You couldn't beat its versatility.
For instance, I've seen it masquerade
as a stole, a motor veil,
most memorably as a makeshift sash,
a rainbow trimming for a boater.
Though who'd have thought
that when we thrashed through
the shades in that draughty mission hall,
its strength would far out-do its quota.

QUARTET

Cheek by jowl,
queer folk saying,
this was where we sat
and read and wrote,
and to the right,
that was the horsehair
one of us died on,
and into the case they say,
this was one of our combs
that one of us dropped
and one hand snatched
from the licks of the fire.
They say our thimble books
are impossible to read.
So. Tiny tales we planted
them like seeds. Agreed.
Jostling sounds in the kitchen,
someone quoting from one of us,
forced brogue in the mouth,
like an apple in the gob of a hog.
Lets rouse the dogs,
go for a ramble.
A mile of purple out
pelt the one with rocks
who dares to ask the question,
When they go will we miss them?

DELIGHT

Walking, thinking about the girls
and how to broach
the world of Christina.
Starkness twists a staid crucifix
of hawthorn,
as from the ground hedges spring
looped and bound
by millions of shiny black beads.
The air whoops, leaves yellow
and bronze, as gentle autumn
purrs the scalps off trees.
Most of them will have pets,
so start with shades of grey delight,
her pencil sketches
of a fox, a wombat, a squirrel.
Chat for a while about teenage
girls and goblins, then silkily
let it slip that they too were sisters.
Let them have their moment of fun,
foraging through gluts of fruit
before peeling back the tap root.

HOMAGE

Tell me again, that story,
the one about Charlotte,
I never tire of hearing it.
Tiny, she stood
patiently waiting.
Staid as a woodblock,
bold print on the cloth
edge of the cemetery.
Sharp as relief on a backdrop,
all black edged and violet.
Indelible. Devoted as the rain,
when through the gates
Christina came, carried,
a scroll on the shoulders of men,
encased in the shell of a beetle,
hard black and bittersweet as jet.

It's true that on the day
Christina passed, leaves tipped,
rose from the heads of trees,
gloves were tugged from every bud,
thorns crossed and cobweb veiled,
and as her kin trundled,
incense swung like monkeys

through wide-eyed branches,
ruffling the heady stoops
of white lilies slanted,
and only once did Charlotte
look back- though in sorrow,
as fame, fame, fame
came purring gently,
brushing herself past her.

CURIO

I take a step back so as not to be seen
and glimpse through a half open door
an old fisher woman knitting.
In her lap unravelled skeins
that look like carrageen
washed up. Strands flounder
between her fingers, hitch a ride
on the backs of her freckled
hands that waft like flat fish through red.
I watch as her eyes scour for weak spots,
or a break in the cable,
and you can just tell by the way
she handles shape that she's not using
the standard wool weight,
and that the four imperfect buttons;
tiny pearlised clippings she's chipped
from inside a South Sea Island shell,
will go perfect down the front when she's done,
and the flight of needles whittled,
stiff by the stove, so I'm told
were made from a redundant baby crib,
though it's said if you look closely
you can see they're more like the ribs
of a whale than spare knitting needles.
Some folk do say they're remnants of Moby.

CHALET

The white brilliance of day
ripples its long white fingers
across a harp string of blue tipped
pines, then rises, sweeps white
the ground before slipping long
into a gown of night.

You sit there staring into the fire.
Won't you turn and look
so I might see what you want from me?
The grate is a menagerie, logs hiss,
 fur cones dribble resin onto a caraway
seeded floor of charred and blackened needles.

Kneeling I rub and pound your feet
as though I' m grinding wheat.
You flinch, kick my hands away,
glide like a seal beneath spearmint,
as I test, test, test you for signs
of weakness, pawing like a polar bear
does the ice flows trembling fontanel.

BRUSHING THE BACK OF YOUR HAND

We sank into our seats as darkness
slotted overhead its final piece,
and grey heaved itself
through the stalls sweeping
its shawl around us as Venice
does in late Autumn.
All I remember is brushing
the back of your hand
as the picture rolled and figures
flickered, and your skin, your skin,
felt scuffed going against its pile,
like velvet or white vellum
on the top of boiled milk,
and I remember thinking,
one day soon, soon
that kind of hand would be mine.

LONGING

Sitting here at the head of the valley
I watch as through the window
fog sinks, comfy into the seat
of a faded dale. All afternoon
I've worried away at myself,
as to how I might sever this longing,
this longing that yearly grows,
unhealthily mutates then multiples.
Outside a woodland bird flies past.
You sent a messenger, to prompt me.
Tear in the fog, and I see you,
see you as you were, that swift
unbearable summer, the two
of us sunning ourselves in the purple
of an orchid studded dale.
You, leaning back, dimming the hazel
in your eyes, laughing off something
flaking about your lashes, soft ash
of a prophesy, for you knew
how it would take hold of me.

HELPING YOU PUT YOUR COAT ON

You half rise, lodge
your trembling knees
like giant sycamore seeds
into the grain of the table.
You butterfly your arms
back for me to catch,
net into its demanding shape,
that shape, that once we had fun
together, trying on.

Now I find myself hovering
like a collector behind you,
whispering to the tender lashings
of the velvet, *go easy, go easy*,
whilst breathless, you writhe,
thrash weakly. Cut down
to size by the sheer spurt of it.

Hopelessly I step in as you slither
your withered arms into the ice silk
hollow of its sleeves,
as first your fingers fumble
with a welt of belt, slip knot.

THE TROUSER SUIT

It hung on the back of the door
staring
at itself in the French bevel,
the fabric,
the pattern,
the fastenings,
the finishing.
Ravishing.

During the preparations
it recalled its first meeting
with warm skin and cold bone.

It chaffed to keep
itself warm
in far off regions
it found remote and desolate.

It liked most to gather
on a fur flower's half
opened petals
leaving its threads
to wane, ripen on wafts
of scent,

serenaded by the strange
internal scores of the body.

It slunk, puckered on its hanger,
when placed with the others,
because its tale was so far
sadly limited.
But it made up
for it and spun
its dreams
for the complete,   —
the co- ordinates
the separates,
about Kashmir
and all the things
its interface
aspired to do.

And thus it was
as the dawn broke,
blotted grey,
it clung fanatic to its thoughts,
like static.

Stripped from its hanger
they took it down
and dressed you in it,
stiffly lowering,
a figurehead-
slotting into the grainy shallows,
the rap of its buttons,
your nipples catching
against the screw,
thud of hardwood.

LETTER

Only now she's gone may we talk freely,
for when she was here she'd partition
herself like a Japanese screen,
all open winged, black lacquered red,
spitting jade and gold between us.
Only now may we take each other
tentatively by the hand, to a side
of her that neither one of us recognises
and make the final pilgrimage,
the two of us coming to an understanding,
interlocked like cattle, bent over words
addressed to both of us, spooling
from a flooded water meadow,
reason after reason from her long letter.

THE GAME

She's here again, I hear her footsteps,
watch as through a broken pane
she strides, swinging bright,
her arms a storm lantern,
down a long neglected path,
crazed and riddled with weeds.
Am I surprised, that she's returned
so soon; has she surprised herself?
In truth I'd given hope up,
and let the garden overthrow itself,
and now her shadow, hand
upon the banister, shuffle on the stair.
I write my name, her name
entwined in dust, a loving cup,
and watch her stand
where moments I once stood.

WALKING IN FOG TO RIBER

They call it fog, only fog.
I let them, for I know better,
better than all of them,
that this is a sign from you
to say you've let your hair
down, for me to wander,
comforted through

deep greys concentrating
in the park, gathering intense
in bold swirls beside
the river's wavy parting.

The insects make hollow sounds,
strumming pale silver,
and dregs of end-of-season ducks
collide on fleeing strands.

Wrapped warm and muffled
I walk until I reach the bridge,
where the ice collects
on the swerve of your scalp,
and your fingers appear,
lifting threads of grey from my eyes,
as your head tosses back,

and I lift my head and look ahead,
and the hillside's bound,
and the dale's a book, a page turned back,
and your hair's back to black streaming,
and your running fast, fast
across the fields to meet me at Riber.

THE BRIDGE

is densely packed,
the sky waxes black.
Two minutes
before midnight
and I'm thinking
of you and how
by a few weeks
you missed
the overlap of centuries.

Revellers push
and in the crush
black drops and
I'm back with you
on the terraces,
the two of us
bending like spoons,
our lips close to supping
the thick soup of the turf.

Overhead the moon
glides lazy like an eye,
bunches of stars smear.

NEW WAVE

If I turned and looked back at us
it would be through French windows,
and the lawn would be swept with snow,
the trees decorated with attitudes of icicles,
and we would be talking intently,
walking purposefully,
each in time with the others step
through tourniquets of breath,
and your arm threaded
through mine would be holding me,
the way you hold a cup brimming,
as if you knew I was that close.
Primed to be thrown
or tossed into the face of something.